Pebble Plus

How to Build a
Fizzy Rocket

Hands-On
SCIENCE
FUN

by Lori Shores

Consulting Editor: Gail Saunders-Smith, PhD

Consultant: Ronald Browne, PhD
Department of Elementary & Early Childhood Education
Minnesota State University, Mankato

CAPSTONE PRESS
a capstone imprint

Pebble Plus is published by Capstone Press,
1710 Roe Crest Drive, North Mankato, Minnesota 56003.
www.capstonepub.com

Library of Congress Cataloging-in-Publication Data
Shores, Lori.
How to build a fizzy rocket / by Lori Shores.
p. cm.—(Pebble plus. Hands-on science fun)
Includes bibliographical references and index.
Summary: "Simple text and full-color photos instruct readers how to build a fizzy rocket and explain the science behind
the activity"—Provided by publisher.
ISBN 978-1-4296-4491-4 (library binding)
ISBN 978-1-4296-5573-6 (paperback)
ISBN 978-1-5435-3590-7 (saddle stitch)
1. Rockets (Aeronautics)—Models—Juvenile literature. I. Title. II. Series.
TL844.S56 2011
621.43'560228—dc22   2009051419

Editorial Credits
Erika L. Shores, editor; Juliette Peters, designer; Sarah Schuette; photo studio specialist; Marcy Morin, scheduler;
  Eric Manske, production specialist

Photo Credits
Capstone Studio/Karon Dubke, all

Artistic Effects: iStockphoto/solos, cover, 1, 2, 3, 22, 23, 24 (starfield design); Otto Rogge Photography, 4-5 (clouds)

Note to Parents and Teachers

The Hands-On Science Fun set supports national science standards related to physical science.
This book describes and illustrates building a fizzy rocket. The images support early readers
in understanding the text. The repetition of words and phrases helps early readers learn new
words. This book also introduces early readers to subject-specific vocabulary words, which are
defined in the Glossary section. Early readers may need assistance to read some words and to
use the Table of Contents, Glossary, Read More, Internet Sites, and Index sections of the book.

Printed in China.
005962

Table of Contents

Safety Note:
Please ask an adult for help in building and launching your fizzy rocket.

Getting Started

Rockets blast off into space. You can use simple materials to launch your own rocket into the air.

Here's what you need:

tape

safety glasses

8.5" x 11" (22 cm x 28 cm)
sheet of paper

scissors

white plastic film canister
with a lid that fits inside
(available anywhere film
is developed)

½ of a fizzing antacid
tablet made with
sodium bicarbonate

1 teaspoon (5 mL) warm water

Making a Fizzy Rocket

Cut the paper in half.

One half will be the body
of the rocket.

Tape the edge of the paper to
the upside down film canister.

Form the paper into a tube.

Tape down the other edge
of paper.

Cut a circle from the other half
of paper. Cut a slit, and overlap
the sides to form a cone.
Tape the cone on top of the tube.

Cut out two triangles, and
tape them to the tube for fins.

Put on safety glasses,
and turn over the rocket.

Then add 1 teaspoon (5 mL)
of warm water to the canister.

Take the rocket, lid,
and antacid outside.

Drop the half tablet
of antacid into the water.

Snap the lid on right away.

Quickly stand up the rocket.

Step back about 6 feet
(2 meters) to watch.

How high will the rocket go?

How Does It Work?

A reaction started when the antacid tablet and water mixed. The water and the tablet made little bubbles of gas.

gas bubbles

Soon the canister filled with gas. Pressure inside the canister made the lid pop off. As gas rushed out, the canister was pushed into the air.

21

Glossary

antacid—a medicine that reduces the amount of acid in your stomach to soothe an upset stomach

fin—a small, triangular structure on a rocket used to help with steering

gas—a substance, such as air, that spreads to fill any space that holds it

launch—to send a rocket into space

material—the thing from which something is made

pressure—a force made by pressing on something

reaction—an action in response to something that happens

Read More

Gibson, Gary. *Making Things Change.* Fun Science Projects. Mankato, Minn.: Stargazer Books, 2009.

Llewellyn, Claire. *Exploring Forces.* A Sense of Science. Mankato, Minn.: Sea-to-Sea, 2009.

Internet Sites

FactHound offers a safe, fun way to find Internet sites related to this book. All of the sites on FactHound have been researched by our staff.

Here's all you do:

Visit *www.facthound.com*

Type in this code: 9781429644914

Index

Word Count: 204
Grade: 1
Early-Intervention Level: 20